PROTEIN POW(D)ER:
The Cookbook

VOLUME I

ANNA SWARD

PROTEIN POW PUBLISHING

Protein Pow Publishing - www.proteinpow.com - Copyright 2013

VOLUME I

First published in Great Britain in 2013 by
Protein Pow Publishing
Suite 515
Regency House
91 Western Road
Brighton
East Sussex
BN1 2NW
United Kingdom
proteinpowdr@gmail.com
www.proteinpow.com

ISBN: 978-0-9573567-0-2

Disclaimer: The author and publisher assume no responsibility or liability whatsoever on the behalf of any purchaser or reader of this cookbook. The author is not a medical doctor, nor does she claim to be. Please consult your primary-care physician before majorly overhauling your diet (particularly if you have medical issues).

Recipes © Anna Sward
Text © Anna Sward
Food Photography © Anna Sward
Illustration © Anna Sward
Cover Photograph © Paul Corkery

A Catalogue in Publication record for this title is available from the British Library.

Printed and bound in Italy by Printer Trento s.r.l.

TO MY PAPA, WHO TAUGHT ME HOW TO FLIP MY PROTEIN PANCAKES.

TABLE OF CONTENTS

INTRODUCTION

This cookbook is the offspring of my blog, www.proteinpow.com, where I chronicle my cooking adventures in the land of protein powder cooking. Over 700 recipes currently live there - recipes for cooking with an array of different protein powders including whey, casein, rice, pea, hemp, egg, beef and all kinds of veggie and dairy-based protein powder blends. Most of my recipes contain less than ten ingredients and follow the same three basic steps: 1. mix together or blend, 2. bake or panfry, 3. frost, allow to set, or cover in melted dark chocolate.

Over the last couple of years, I have taken down a number of my best recipes from the blog to include them in this cookbook in order to illustrate how, by thinking outside the shake, all sorts of magical foods can be brought to life. I want to show you how, by using protein powders, nutritionally void or suboptimal categories of foods - foods commonly containing hydrogenated fats, preservatives, sugars and refined carbohydrates - can feature in our healthy diets without a side dish of 'I shouldn't have.' You see, protein powder cooking allows you to enjoy these foods with gusto. In a way, it lets you 'have your cake and eat it too'! All you have to do is turn these foods on their head by giving them a nutritious makeover: out with simple carbs, in with protein; out with preservatives, in with fresh ingredients; out with empty calories, in with wholesome foods. And the best thing of all? That anyone can do it - no special skills are required. All you need are some basic ingredients, a pan, an oven, mixing bowls, a handheld blender, mixer or food processor, and... you're good to go!

All the recipes you see in this cookbook (as well as on my blog) have been cooked, photographed, and eaten by yours truly. What you see, in other words, is completely what you get. I have included little blurbs alongside some of the recipes here, introducing a bit of commentary to give you an insight into how each the recipe was born and/or how it turned out. I should also mention that the cartoon drawings you'll find dispersed throughout this cookbook (barring of course The Muffin Man on page 52 and the crocodile on page 91) are not random - they're my blog's readers, personal friends, and people who've inspired me and made an impact on the creation and development of this cookbook (e.g. Ben, Katie, Nic, Vitor, Ash, Matt, Thomas, Dude, Kim, Paul, and Will). You'll also find suggestions for substitutions alongside many of my ingredients so you can tweak the recipes as you see fit. Remember that cooking times can vary depending on which powders you use, what kind of oven you have, and the level of elevation you're in! So always keep an eye on everything you bake :-)

In the next three pages you will find three charts: one for protein powder substitutions, one for ingredient substitutions, and a conversion chart for commonly-used measurements. I have included these charts here to show you how you can play around with your protein powders and to guide you through the recipes found in this cookbook. Alongside each recipe, I have also included macronutrients (or 'macros') per serving. Underneath these 'macros', you'll find that I have broken down each recipe by kcals (calories), grams of protein, grams of carbohydrates (or 'carbs'), grams of fat, and grams of fiber.

With this cookbook, a whole new world you may not have even known existed will open up before you: a world of exciting high-protein cooking where your taste buds, your health, and your fitness reign supreme! So welcome to the party, make yourself at home, and when you're done working your way through the recipes in this book? Log on to proteinpow.com for an endless stream of more!

PROTEIN POWDER SUBSTITUTIONS

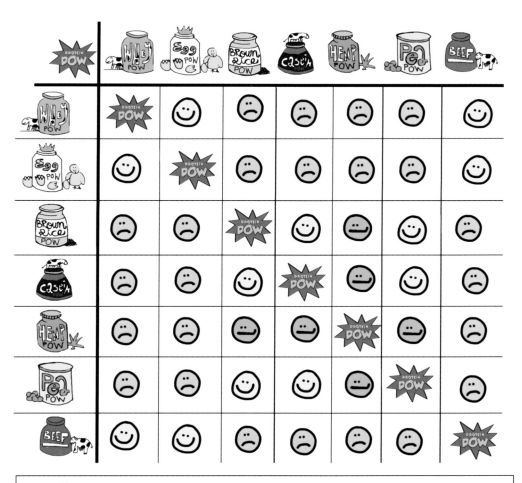

INGREDIENT SUBSTITUTIONS

IMPORTANT NOTE: You'll note that I use a lot of cartoned coconut milk in my recipes - by 'cartoned coconut milk' I mean the low-calorie coconut milk that's commonly sold in a carton as a substitute for regular cow's milk. I don't mean canned coconut milk as this has a totally different consistency and is much higher in kcals and fat. If you'd like to replace cartoned coconut milk in any of the recipes found here or in my blog, I suggest you do it with a nut milk (like almond or hazelnut milk), rice milk, or just good old-fashioned dairy milk.

BASIC CONVERSION CHART (CUPS/SPOONS to GRAMS)

I decided to write this cookbook using cup and spoon measurements, instead of grams, because I find the former far easier to visualize and to follow - you don't need any kitchen scales or weighing units to recreate these recipes. All you need is a set of measuring cups and spoons. If you work in grams and want to get a feel for what cups and spoons roughly amount to, here's a basic conversion chart of some of the most common ingredients you'll find in this cookbook:

	PROTEIN POWDER	COCONUT FLOUR	EGG WHITES	OATS
1 TSP	2.3	6.25	8.3	4
1 TBSP	7	12.5	16.7	8
1/8 CUP	14	25	33.5	16
1/4 CUP	28	50	67	32
1/2 CUP	56	100	134	64
1 CUP	112	200	268	128

ORGANIC WHEY PROTEIN BREAD

INGREDIENTS

1/4 cup of unsweetened (organic) whey protein powder
3/4 cup of liquid egg whites
1/4 cup of apple and peach (or just apple) puree
1/2 cup of quinoa flakes
1/2 cup of amaranth flour
1/8 cup of seed mix (pumpkin seeds + flaxseeds + sunflower seeds)
1 tsp of baking powder
1 tsp of sea salt

DIRECTIONS

Blend all ingredients together and bake the batter inside two small bread-loaf tins for about 30-35 minutes at 160 C (320 F). If you want to make a bigger loaf, just pour all the mix into a regular sized bread tin (and adjust cooking times accordingly). Once baked, remove from the oven, let the bread cool, and... boom! Slice and sandwich it up with your favorite fillings!

See the next page for a few sandwich filling ideas ;-)

Sandwich Filling Ideas

Ham and mayo (one of my favorites)
Thinly sliced cucumber and grass-fed butter
Bacon, lettuce, and tomato (a classic)
Peanut butter and melted dark chocolate
Turkey, avocado, mayo and mature cheddar
Tuna, mayo, paprika, and green chile powder
Roast beef and grass-fed butter
Hummus and sliced egg
Goat cheese and brie

MACROS

Per one small loaf out of the two you get from
the mix above: 354kcals, 27g protein, 41g carbs
(6.7g sugars), 9.4g fat (1.2g sat) and 7g of fiber!

ROSEMARY & SAFFRON PROTEIN BREAD

When I made this bread, I almost crushed my head against the ceiling by levitating in pleasure as I ate it. It was not only absurdly delicious, it also powered one hell of a gym-sesssion, KAPOOOW! This is protein powder bread-baking at its finest. Just remember, when you eat this: watch your head ;-)

INGREDIENTS

1 cup of liquid egg whites
1/2 cup of saffron water (i.e. boiling water left to cool with a couple strands of saffron)
1/2 cup of organic whey protein powder (plain i.e. unsweetened)
1 cup of gluten-free oats (can sub this with quinoa or millet flakes)
1/8 cup of chestnut flour
1 tbsp dried (or fresh!) rosemary
1 tbsp of coconut flour
1 tsp of baking soda

DIRECTIONS

Blend all the ingredients together and bake your batter in a small bread pan at 160 C (320 F) for about 35 minutes or until, when stabbed with a knife, your knife comes out clean. With some organic grass-fed butter on top... oy! It's amazing :-D

MACROS

Per one loaf (out of which you can get 12 slices like those pictured here): 609kcals, 53g protein, 74g carbs (10.5g sugars), 9.6g fat (3g sat), and 15g fiber!

VANILLA WHEY PROTEIN PANCAKES

INGREDIENTS

1 cup of liquid egg whites
1/2 cup of vanilla whey protein powder
1/4 cup of pumpkin puree
1/4 cup of gluten-free oat flour
1/8 cup of ground almonds
1/2 tsp of sea salt
2 tsps of coconut oil

DIRECTIONS

Blend everything together except for the coconut oil. Add the coconut oil to a non-stick pan and turn on the heat to HIGH. When the heat is high enough that the coconut oil begins to sizzle, spoon your pancake batter on the pan. You can do like I did and make little ones or you can make two giant pan-sized pancakes. Flip (ideally in the air) and BAAAM: they're ready to be devoured :-D

MACROS

Per 14 small (aka 'dollar') pancakes: 514kcals, 50g protein, 36g carbs (8g sugars), 19g fat (4g sat) and 8.6g fiber.

VANILLA
COCONUT
PROTEIN
PANCAKES

INGREDIENTS   DIRECTIONS   MACROS

INGREDIENTS

1/4 cup of vanilla egg white protein powder
1 cup of semi-skimmed milk
3/4 cup of rolled oats
1/4 cup of coconut flour
1 medium frozen (or fresh) banana

DIRECTIONS

Blend all the ingredients together and fry up your batter on a non-stick pan further non-sticked with a couple tsps of coconut oil. You get nine small pancakes out of the batter which, trust me, is a lot! So consider sharing with one or two other people!

MACROS

Per nine small pancakes: 822kcals, 56g of protein, 96g of carbs (43g sugars), 20g of fat (11g sat), and 18g of fiber.

ORANGE PROTEIN PANCAKES

INGREDIENTS

1/2 boiled orange
1/4 cup of ground almonds
1/4 cup of whey protein powder (toffee or vanilla flavored)
1 tbsp of coconut flour
2 whole eggs

DIRECTIONS

First, you've got to get an orange, wash it, and boil it - whole. Yeah, with the peel and all. I know it sounds strange but trust me, it's amazing! Try this recipe and you'll see what I mean.

After you've boiled your orange for about ten minutes and it's super soft (soft like I-can-cut-it-with-a-knife-and-it-feels-as-soft-as-butter), take it out and cut off the orange's top and bottom. Then, slice it in half and de-seed (if it has seeds) and blend 1/2 of it with the rest of the ingredients. Finally, just pan-fry your batter on a non-stick pan (further non-sticked with PAM or coconut oil) like regular pancakes! Top with maple syrup or your pancake topping of choice.

Seriously, don't be intimidated by the idea of eating an unpeeled boiled orange, it's fine. Oh, it's more than fine - it's incredible! Just try it out and see for yourself :-)

NOTE: Now, this recipe uses half of the orange. Make sure you save the other half to make it again!

MACROS

Per six small pancakes or two big ones: 435kcals, 34g protein, 16g carbs (10.7g sugars), 26g fat (4g sat), 6g fiber.

This is one of those recipes that made my heart go crazy with excitement when I first made it. It's just so fun and tasty! And oh, to have a crunchy protein cereal! It's like a dream come true to me :-D And it lasts for a few days in a plastic bag too, covering not one but several of your breakfasts. What's not to love? Sugar-free, nutritious, high in protein, and high in fiber! It's amazing in a bowl of almond milk too :-D

PROTEIN CEREAL

This recipe is open to lots of variations. For example, you can add some nut butter or some actual chopped nuts to the mixture (if you are into nutty cereals). You can also add some grated coconut to it (if you're feeling tropical); you can add raisins (if you're into cereal with raisins) or, well, you can add whatever. Just make this cereal yours! Enjoy it :-)

INGREDIENTS

1/4 cup of millet flakes
1/4 cup of vanilla brown rice protein powder
1/2 tbsp of 'fitness fiber'
(or psyllium husks)
3/4 cup of liquid egg whites

MACROS

Per one serving (out of two because the above ingredients yield two good-sized bowls of cereal):

141kcals
16.5g protein
23g carbs (0.7g sugars)
1.5g fat (0.2g sat)
6g fiber!

DIRECTIONS

First, blend all the ingredients together and spread the batter on a cookie tray as flat as possible. Then, stick it under the oven grill for 10-15 minutes, until it cooks and begins to get golden brown. Take it out from under the grill and proceed to break it apart into small pieces. You can do this by hand, like I did, or with a knife (cutting it with a knife will allow you to end up with 'neater' looking cereal pieces; I did it by hand to end up with more cornflakey-looking cereal). After you do this, stick it back under the grill for a good ten minutes, shaking the tray every five or so minutes to ensure the cereal browns and crunches-up evenly.

Note: Big thank you to Nicola who, at BFIT 2012, inspired me to create this recipe!

PROTEIN MINI— DONUTS

There NEEDS to be a time in your near future when you too break the fast with a bowl of protein mini-donuts. There's nothing more exciting than piling them on your spoon and/or eating them one by one after submerging them in milk while taking in the fact that yes, you ARE eating a bowl full of donuts! Food like this, ahhhh, it makes the child within happy :-)

INGREDIENTS

2 egg whites
2 cooked beetroots (sub this with cooked
sweet potato if beetroot is your nemesis and/
or you simply don't like it enough to want to
include its subtle sweetness)
1/2 cup of vanilla brown rice protein powder
1/2 tbsp of toffee flavdrops or your sweetener
of choice (this is optional but nice as it adds
an extra element of sweetness to the whole
thing)
1 square (10 grams) of dark chocolate

DIRECTIONS

Blend all your ingredients together (except for the chocolate) and bake the batter in a mini donut silicone tray for about 20 minutes at 160 C (320 F). When your donuts are ready, all you do is grab a square of dark chocolate (I used 100% dark chocolate because I wanted to keep the donuts sugar free and deeply darrrrk) and massage the top of each donut as soon as they come out of the oven. The chocolate will melt 'on impact' with the hot donut, creating a delicious chocolate shell on top!

MACROS

For a bowl of cereal, I normally use five to ten donuts. Macros per donut (and be amazed because these babies are very low cal and high protein):

15.3kcals
2.7g protein
0.8g carbs (0.1g sugars)
0.2g fat (0.1g sat)
0.4g fiber

BURIED BANANA PROTEIN BREAD

INGREDIENTS

1/2 cup of pumpkin puree (or a cooked sweet potato)
1/2 cup of vanilla whey protein powder
1 cup of liquid egg whites
2 bananas (one for the batter and another banana to bury inside)
1/2 cup of coconut flour
3/8 cup of rolled oats
1 tsp of cinnamon (optional but highly recommended)

DIRECTIONS

Blend all ingredients together (except for the second banana) and pour them in a bread loaf pan. Then, grab the remaining banana and bury it STRAIGHT into the center of your batter until it's fully covered. Bake at 160 C (320 F) for about 40 minutes or until, when stabbing it with a knife, the knife comes out clean.

MACROS

Per one slice (out of the ten you get from the mix): 96kcals, 8.1g protein, 12.1g carbs (4.9g sugars), 1.3g fat (0.7g sat), and 3.2g fiber!

MULTIBERRY
PROTEIN
BREAD

INGREDIENTS

1 cup of liquid egg whites
1 cup of unflavored pea protein powder
1/2 cup of buckwheat flour
1/4 cup of dried mulberries (or dates)
1 cup of coconut milk
1/2 tbsp of stevia
1/ tsp of baking powder
1/2 cup of goji berries
1/2 cup of frozen blueberries

DIRECTIONS

Blend all ingredients together (except for the berries.) Then, add the berries, mix the batter with a spoon (so as to keep the berries whole), and bake it for about 40 minutes at 160 C (320 F). When your loaf comes out of the oven, let it cool. Then, cut yourself a slice or three, spread some organic grass-fed butter on top and, oh, oh, oh! Experience a whole cascade of NOM-MMMMMM!!!!

MACROS

Per one slice (out of 10):
76kcals
8.6g protein
8.5g carbs (3.2g sugars)
0.9g fat (0.4g sat)
1.1g fiber

INGREDIENTS

3/4 cup of liquid egg whites
1/2 cup of organic whey protein (unflavored or vanilla)
1/2 cup of quinoa flakes (can sub this with millet flakes, ground almonds, or ground oats)
1/8 cup of coconut flour
1tsp of baking powder
1 tbsp of vanilla essence
1 tbsp of cinnamon
1 medium carrot - grated and added AFTER the above is blended together
1/2 tbsp of stevia (optional but nice)

DIRECTIONS

Blend together all ingredients and bake for about 30-35 minutes at 160 C (320 F). I baked the batter in a bread loaf tin because I wanted to slice it but feel free to bake it in a cake pan if you want to end up with nice triangular slices of cake. The final product was great, especially topped with cream cheese and/or almond butter!

MACROS

Per one slice (out of ten): 68.7kcals, 6.6g protein, 7g carbs (5g sugars), 1.2g fat (0.5g sat), and 2.2 g fiber.

CHOCOLATE & PEANUT BUTTER PROTEIN BREAD

INGREDIENTS

1 whole egg
2 egg whites
1/2 cup of chocolate whey protein powder
1/4 cup of pumpkin puree
1/2 cup of whole milk
3/4 cup of oats
1 tbsp cocoa
1 tbsp coconut flour
1 tbsp peanut butter
1 tsp baking soda
1 tsp stevia

DIRECTIONS

Blend all ingredients together and bake for 35-40 minutes at 160 C (320 F). You can bake in a big cake pan or in a bread pan, like I did, if you want to end up with bread-shaped slices of cake. Consider topping it with nut butter, regular butter, or chocolate spread – it's delicious!

Per one slice out of ten: 101.1kcals, 6.5g protein, 10.7g carbs (0.6g sugars), 3.5g fat (1.3g sat), and 1.8g fiber

I solemnly and sincerely declare that the recipe below, if followed in its entirely, shall bring to your life a batch of exquisite, wholly delectable and nothing short of heavenly protein muffins. I swear, under each and every god of Mount Olympus, that it is one of the best protein muffins I've ever made (and I've made a LOT). But please, don't take my word for it. Make them. Make them and weep!

CHOCOLATE PROTEIN MUFFIN

INGREDIENTS

1 can of pumpkin puree
4 fresh egg whites
1 whole egg
2 tbsp of 100% cocoa
3 pitted medjool dates
1/2 cup of unflavored (or chocolate) whey protein powder
1/2 cup of millet flakes
1/2 cup of goji berries
1/2 cup of milk (I used chocolate coconut milk but any milk will do)
1 tbsp of stevia
1/2 tbsp of baking soda
1 square of dark and/or white chocolate (optional but recommended)

DIRECTIONS

Blend all ingredients together and place the mix inside your muffin cases with a couple of blueberries on top of each muffin. Bake at 160 C (320 F) for about 35 minutes or until your knife comes out clean after you stab the muffins. Take them out of the oven as soon as they cook (you don't want to overcook them because then they run the risk of getting dry). So, basically, as soon as your knife or fork comes out clean when you stab the muffins, bam -> take them out of the oven.

What I then did was stick a small square of 90% dark chocolate and 1/4 square of white chocolate inside each hot muffin. The chocolate began melting inside at once, I could see it slowly start to escape the muffin and... *gulp*... it was just... amazing.

 Per one out of twelve without the chocolate inside (because this is optional; they were gorgeous without it too): 89kcals, 7.5g protein, 12g carbs (7.4g sugars), 1.7g fat, and 1.4g fiber.

THE AMAZING PINK PROTEIN NUFFINS

I think you will LOVE these muffins - they are soft, fluffy, moist, light, almost buttery and extremely tasty with bit of actual butter on top. Macro-wise too, they are superb! And are you wondering why they are pink? That's because I used a LOT of artificial pink food coloring.

Hehe, of course not ;-)

They are pink because I used beetroot. Before you break into infernal screams of the "PLEASE! NO BEETROOT!" variety, I just want to say that they don't taste of beetroot. In fact, I masked the beetroot flavor here like a first-class wizard, bringing it down several notches and turning it into nothing more than a suggestion beneath the strong and fervent power of toffee and vanilla!

INGREDIENTS

1 container of low-fat cottage cheese (250g)
2 cooked beetroots
1/2 cup of vanilla whey protein powder
1 whole egg
2 egg whites
1/4 cup of coconut flour
1/4 cup of buckwheat flour
1 tbsp of toffee flavdrops
1 tbsp of vanilla essence
1 tsp of baking powder

DIRECTIONS

Blend together all the ingredients and bake the batter at 160 C (320 F) for about 35 minutes inside seven silicone muffin cases. Remove them as soon as they're cooked through, let them cool and then... boom! Devour :-D

MACROS

Per muffin: 119kcals, 15.4g protein, 7.5g carbs (1.4g sugars), 2g fat (1.4g sat), and 3.2g fiber

When I made these protein muffins, I wasn't sure what the result would be. I mean, making muffins with... melon? But then I took a bite and whoa, they blew me away! I rate this recipe as one of my all-time favorites. The muffins are soft, moist, and mmm... just try them and you'll see :-D

Melon PROTEIN Muffins

INGREDIENTS

1/4 cup of vanilla whey protein powder
1 cup of liquid egg whites
1/4 cup of vanilla brown rice protein powder
1/2 fresh melon (cantaloupe)
1 tsp baking powder
1/2 cup of oats

DIRECTIONS

Blend all ingredients together and bake the batter inside muffin cases for about 35 minutes at 170 C (338 F). Then, if you want an even crazier taste experience, top them with a tiny bit of organic grass-fed butter as soon as they come out of the oven. Protein life doesn't get any better than that!

MACROS

Per one muffin - out of the seven you get from the mix above: 106.7kcals, 12.7g protein, 9.8g carbs (3.6g sugars), 1.55g fat (0.7g sat), and 3.1g fiber!

MACROS Per one donut cake (out of the three you get from the mix here if you choose to use the same molds I did): 252kcals, 31g protein, 7g carbs, 11.1g fat, and 0.7g fiber.

INGREDIENTS

3/4 cup of liquid egg whites
1/2 cup of cocoa powder
1/2 cup of unflavored (or chocolate) whey protein powder
1 medium cooked beetroot
1/4 cup of unflavored (or chocolate) pea protein powder
1 tbsp of toffee flavdrops
1/4 cup of goat cream (or regular cream)
1.5 squares of 100% dark chocolate

DIRECTIONS

Blend all ingredients together and bake your batter in three (ideally silicone) cake moulds (they can be round, bundt shaped like mine or just regular, large muffin cases) for about 20 minutes at 170 C (332 F) or until, when poked with a kinfe, the knife comes out clean.

When they come out of the oven, turn them over right away and 'massage' the top of each one (which will be piping hot) with a square and a half of 100% dark chocolate (i.e. 15 grams-worth of dark chocolate.) The chocolate will melt upon contact when you do it this way (so you don't have to melt it and pour it over them). Why the chocolate on top? Because it gives them a shell which is *cuhrayze* good! You don't HAVE to top them with chocolate if you don't want to though, I'm just a sucker for chocodarkness and wanted to add an extra touch of OOMPH!

CHOCOLATE CAKE PROTEIN DONUTS

VANILLA PROTEIN BLONDIES

 **MACROS** Out of the six squares you get from the mix above (without the almond butter in the center): 103kcals, 6.2g carbs (2g sugars), 9.4g protein, 3.8g fat (1g sat), and 1g fiber.

INGREDIENTS

1/4 cup of ground almonds
4 tbsp of (unflavored or vanilla) pea protein powder
1/4 cup of milk (whole)
1 whole egg
1/2 cup of liquid egg whites
1/2 cup of oats
1/4 cup of vanilla casein protein powder
1/2 tbsp of coffee substitute
1/2 tbsp of coconut flour
3/4 tsp of baking soda

DIRECTIONS

Using a handheld blender or mixer, blend all ingredients together. Bake the batter in a brownie tin at 170 C (338 F) for about 35 minutes or until, when you stab the blondies with a knife, your knife comes out clean. When they're done, remove them from the oven and let them cool. Then, cut them into squares and then horizontally slice them to fill them with almond butter or peanut butter or sunflower seed butter or even jam! This is optional, of course, but they complement the blondies' flavor and add some nice extra texture so ... give it a shot with and without :-)

CHOCOLATE PROTEIN
MINI DONUTS

INGREDIENTS

1 large cooked sweet potato
1 cup of liquid egg whites
1/2 cup of whey protein powder (vanilla or white chocolate flavored)
1/4 cup of unflavored or vanilla pea protein powder
2 tbsp of coconut flour
6 squares of dark chocolate

DIRECTIONS

Blend all ingredients together and bake for around 15-20 minutes at 170 C (338 F) in a silicone mini donut tray; you'll get 36 mini donuts. When they come out of the oven, let them cool, and proceed to melt 60g of 100% dark chocolate in a *bain marie* (i.e. a glass bowl on top of a pot of boiling water). Once the chocolate has melted, grab each donut and dip the top (or all of it, it's up to whether you want a half covered or a fully covered donut) into the chocolate. Once you've coated all your donuts, transfer them to the freezer for 10 minutes or to the fridge for 20 (to allow the chocolate to set). Aaaaaand... that's it. You're done. Consider doing what I do with the donuts on pages 26-29. In other words, treat them as 'cereal'! It's seriously a blast :-D

MACROS

Per one mini donut (out of 36): 24.2kcals, 1.78g carbs (0.5g sugars), 2.32g protein, 1g fat (0.7g sat), and 0.61g fiber!

DAD'S PROTEIN CHEESECAKE

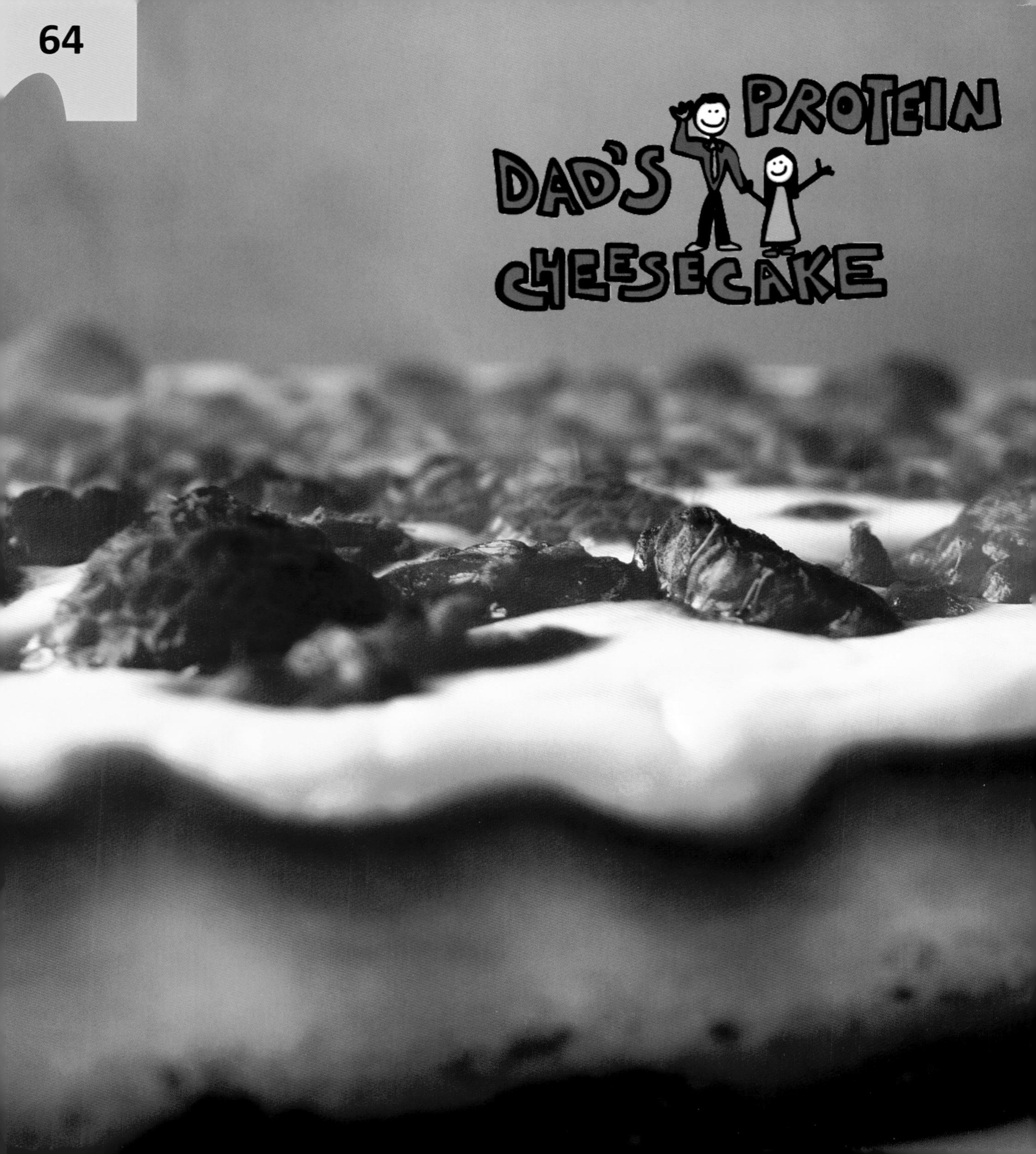

I have an amazing dad and this cheesecake is proudly dedicated to him because he loves protein cheesecake and raspberries! So, here's to you, Pa! A recipe for one of the best protein cheese-cakes I've ever made :-)

INGREDIENTS

For the base:
1 and 3/4 cups of slivered almonds
2 medjool dates
1.5 tbsps of sunflower seed butter
1 tsp of wattleseeds (or dates)

For the cheesecake filling :
1 container (250g) of quark (could sub with cream cheese, or cottage cheese, or Greek yogurt)
3 tbsp of vanilla egg white protein powder
1 cup of whole milk
5 tbsp of vanilla casein protein powder

MACROS

Per slice (if you divide the cheesecake into eight slices): 189kcals, 13g protein, 11g carbs (4.9g sugars), 11g fat (1.2g sat), and 2.2g fiber!

DIRECTIONS

Blend together all the base ingredients and press the ensuing mix into a pie tray before baking at 170 C (338 F) for about 15 minutes or until the base has cooked through and browned nicely. Take it out of the oven and allow it to cool. Then, blend all the cheesecake ingredients together to create a creamy batter and pour this batter on top of the base, finishing the whole thing by adding one cup of fresh raspberries on top. Bake this for about 30 minutes at 160 C (320 F). Remember, when you do this, to keep an eye on it and take it out as SOON as it feels taut when you press it lightly with your finger. You really don't want to over-bake it because then you'll end up with a weird cousin of cheesecake that'll give you sadface and we don't want THAT. When it's done, let it cool, grab a chair, sit down, cut yourself a slice, take out a fork or spoon, dig in and........ mmmm :-)

APPLE & VANILLA PROTEIN TOWERS

When I was little, I used to make my dad build me huge towers out of lego - and I mean GIANT towers - just so I could run into them and bulldoze them with immense amounts of joy. Here I am now, twenty-some years later, building my own towers (this time, of protein) and equally demolishing them with gusto. Long live childhood memories and their adult manifestations, eh?

Anyways, I made the cake part of this tower by baking my ingredients in a round cake pan, before cutting off the edges (and eating them). I cut off the edges because I wanted to end up with four little squares to then stack and interlayer with protein frosting. The illustration on the right here shows you what I did.

INGREDIENTS

1/2 an apple (with or without skin)
1/2 cup of vanilla brown rice protein powder
1/2 cup of coconut water
1/4 cup of 0% fat Greek yogurt
1/2 cup of oat flour
2 tsp of roasted wattleseed (if you don't have access to this, don't worry about it, just omit it or sub with dates)
2 tsp of cinnamon
2 tsp of toffee flavdrops

The frosting I made by mixing: 1/2 cup of 0% fat Greek yogurt + 1/4 cup of vanilla whey protein + 2 tbsp of vanilla casein and sticking that between layers of cake :-)

MACROS

Per one tower: 445kcals, 70g protein, 35g carbs (8g sugars), 3.5g fat (1.4g sat), and 5.2g fiber.

I created this recipe to commemorate the blog's first birthday. It combines two of my favorite flavors - chocolate and vanilla - and also has this extra layer of melted chocolate on top which AAAAA!!!! I made seven of these (to share) using a mini-bread tin. If you don't have this though, feel free to use seven muffin cases or bake the batter inside a cheesecake pan for more of a cheesecakey-cake! Just play around with the recipe and enjoy :-)

CHOCOLATE & VANILLA LAYERED CAKE ^ PROTEIN

INGREDIENTS

For the chocolate protein bases, blended together:

1 whole apple (de-seeded)
1 tbsp of rolled oats
1/4 cup of quinoa flakes
1 tbsp of almond butter
1/4 cup of brown rice protein powder (chocolate or unflavored)
2 tsp of toffee flavdrops
1/2 cup of liquid egg whites
2 tsp of cocoa powder

For the vanilla protein top, blended together:

1 container of Greek yogurt (200g)
1 cup of liquid egg whites
1/2 cup of vanilla whey protein powder
2 tbsp of ricotta cheese
2 tsbp of oat flour

DIRECTIONS

Blend all your base ingredients together and bake for ten minutes in a mini loaf pan (you could also bake this in a regular bread, brownie, or cake pan... or even in muffin cases) at 180 C (356 F). Then, pour the vanilla mix on top of the bases and stick them back in the oven for 15-20 minutes at the same temperature. Make sure you keep an eye on them and don't let them overcook. Take them out as SOON as your knife comes out clean (you want the cakes to be moist and not overly bready). Finally, melt a bit of chocolate on top by rubbing it on the hot cakes. This is optional BUT highly recommended :-)

MACROS

Per one mini cake out of seven: 177kcals, 17g protein, 11g carbs (3g sugars), 7g fat (1g sat), and 2g fiber!

INGREDIENTS

For the cake:
2 cooked beetroots
1/2 cup of chocolate hemp protein powder
2 tbsp of unflavored pea protein powder
3/4 cup of liquid egg whites
1/4 cup of cocoa powder
1 cup of cartoned coconut milk
1/4 cup of peanut flour

For the frosting:
1/4 cup of hemp protein powder
1/4 cup of chocolate casein
3/4 cup of cartoned coconut milk

MACROS

Per slice (if you slice the cake into eight): 145.8kcals, 17.2g protein, 8g carbs (3.1g sugars), 4.8g fat (1.3g sat) and 4.7g fiber.

DIRECTIONS

First, blend all above ingredients together and bake the batter in a cake pan at 170 C (338 F) for about 30 minutes or until your knife comes out clean. Then, for the frosting, just mix together all the ingredients in a bowl (using a spoon or whisker). Then, place the mix in a plastic bag with a piping nozzle sticking out of one corner. You could use a piping bag for the job but a sandwich bag with a hole cut at one corner for the nozzle does the job :-) Finally, add your frosting to the top of the cake and the sides and... kapow! Done :-)

Note: If you want to see how I frost my protein cakes using a piping nozzle, check out my videos at: youtube.com/proteinpow.

MAPLENESS PROTEIN CAKE

The first thing I should mention is that this cake contains no maple syrup. Why 'Mapleness' then? Because of the mulberries. You see, the first time I tried baking with mulberries I was shocked at how sweet and 'maple-syrupy' they were. I thought I'd unveiled one of the world's best kept food secrets: that mapleness exists beyond the maple tree; that it can be found in one type of dried berry that, when pressed, squeezed, blended, mashed, or eaten whole, yields a deep and sweet flavor reminiscent of the famous syrup! Served with some (protein) ice cream, this cake was an absolute sweet sensation! So I urge you to get some mulberries and give it a shot because mmmm, its mapleness will surprise you too :-)

INGREDIENTS

1 whole egg
1 egg white
1/2 cup of canned chickpeas
1/4 cup of vanilla egg white protein powder
1 large banana
1/4 cup of almond milk
1/2 up of ground almonds
1/2 cup of mulberries
1 tbsp of apple fiber
1 tsp of baking soda
1/2 tsp of cinnamon
1 tbsp of vanilla essence

DIRECTIONS

Blend all ingredients together and bake them in a round cake pan at 150 C (302 F) for about 35 minutes or until cooked through. Let the cake cool, cut yourself a slice, top it with almond or peanut butter and oooooh!

MACROS

Per one slice (if you slice it into eight): 85.25kcals, 9.25g carbs (2.8g sugar), 6g protein, 2.8g fat, and 1.8g fiber!

INGREDIENTS

1 cup of chocolate hemp protein powder
1/2 cup of pumpkin puree
1 cup of liquid egg whites
3 tbsp of coconut flour
1/2 cup of buckwheat flour
1/4 cup of apple and blueberry baby puree (or plain old applesauce)
1/2 cup of cartoned coconut milk
1/3 of a bar of dark chocolate

DARK CHOCOLATE PROTEIN CAKE

DIRECTIONS

Blend all ingredients together and bake in a round cake pan at 160 C (320 F) for about 40 minutes or until your knife comes out clean. Then, as SOON as your cake is done, take it out and grab 1/3 of a bar of dark chocolate. Cut this up into pieces and 'massage' the cake with the chocolate. Basically, as you do this, the chocolate melts around the cake, creating a coverture of goodness. This technique works a treat and you get the added bonus of watching the chocolate slowly melt on the cake. I added a tbsp of goats cream on top of my slice and, oh! What a revolution! It was the PERFECT combination! Absolutely mad, this whole thing... pure and undistilled chocolate deliciousness on a plate. Try it :-)

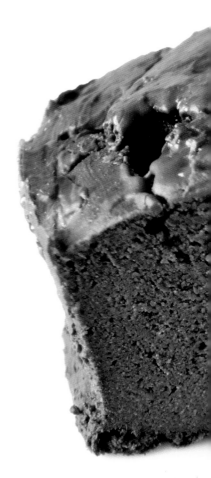

MACROS

Per slice (out of the eight I got from the mix above):
154kcals, 13g protein, 15g carbs (3.7g sugars), 4.8g fat (1.1g sat), and 6.4g fiber!

BANANA FILLED PROTEIN TRUFFLES

INGREDIENTS

1/4 cup of vanilla whey/casein protein powder
1/8 cup of oat flour
3 tbsps of peanut butter
1/8 cup of cartoned coconut milk (or enough to bind it all together)
6 freeze-dried bananas
4 squares of dark chocolate (80%)

MACROS

I made a dozen small truffles. You could make a few larger ones or even turn them into protein bars! For mine though, 1 out of 12 contained, approximately: 86.9kcals, 3.7g carbs (1.15g sugars), 4.5g protein, 6.75g fat (2g sat), and 1.45g fiber.

DIRECTIONS

Mix all the ingredients together, except the bananas and the chocolate. You can mix all the stuff using a fork (this is better than using a blender because the mix will be sticky and you don't want to end up with a ton of it stuck to the bottom of the blender). When your mixture becomes 'pasty' and dry enough to shape with your hands, divide it into six and put a freeze-dried banana in the center as you roll the mix into a ball. Then, melt the chocolate in a *bain marie* (i.e. a glass bowl on top of a pot of boiling water). When the chocolate has melted, dip the protein balls in there (using a spoon) and then place them on a sheet of baking paper. When all the truffles are done, stick them in the freezer for 15-20 minutes. Then, take them out, grab one, bite in, feel the crunch of the banana, the sweetness of the chocolate, and oh! Savor their deliciousness :-D

COCOA & PROTEIN ESPRESSO BEANS

INGREDIENTS

1/4 cup of espresso beans
1/4 cup of chocolate whey protein powder
3/4 bar of dark chocolate
1/8 cup of cocoa powder

Note: Remember to use decaffeinated beans if you plan on having a bunch of these (especially in the late afternoon/evening or night!) I made the mistake of eating a bunch one evening and must have counted three million sheep before I finally fell asleep...

DIRECTIONS

This recipe is SUPER easy. You just need to follow three steps: Step 1: Melt your chocolate in a *bain marie* (i.e. a glass bowl on top of a pot of boiling water). Step 2: Once melted, mix the whey into the chocolate (or the chocolate into the whey) and throw your coffee beans in there to coat them. Step 3: Roll the chocolate and whey covered espresso beans in a bunch of cocoa powder and transfer them to the fridge for an 30 minutes. That's it!

Per half serving of ALL the beans: 151kcals, 8.35g carbs, 20.8g protein, 16.5g fat, and 4.85g fiber!

I don't know about you, but I'm absolutely against the idea of buying protein bars. I find that most store-bought bars are not only a huge waste of money, but when they're not candy bars in disguise full of XYZs, they're unpalatable and/or impossible to pleasurably chew. Better to make one's own, I always say. Because homemade protein bars are a whole lot cheaper, are easy to make, and are waaay better - better tasting and better for you! So here's a recipe to get you started; a recipe for one of the most popular protein bar recipes on proteinpow.com ;-)

A word of warning though: once you try these bars, you'll never want to buy a protein bar again!

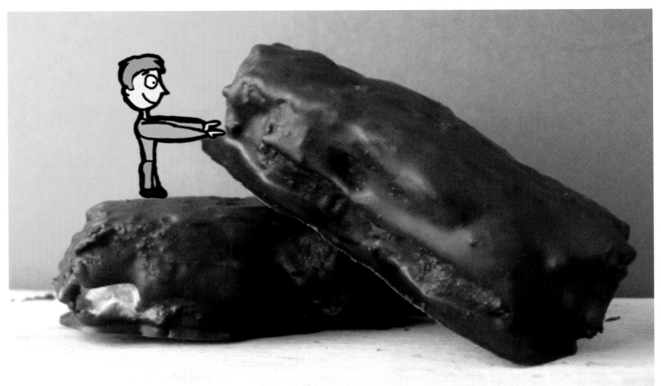

INGREDIENTS

1/2 cup of vanilla whey protein powder
1/4 cup of toasted coconut (just toast some coconut flakes in a skillet; it makes them even tastier!)
1/4 cup of coconut flour (could sub with ground almonds too)
1/4 cup of milk (I used cow's semi-skimmed but coconut or almond milk would be great here as well)
About a 1/3 of a bar of dark chocolate

MACROS

Per one bar (out of the three you get from the mix above): 212kcals, 16.6g protein, 8.8g carbos, 13g fat, and 6g fiber!

DIRECTIONS

Step 1: Mix the above ingredients in a bowl (except for the chocolate) and divide the mixture into three. You'll notice the mix is nice and compact. Feel free to eat some of the batter at this stage. If it's too fiberful, add some ground nuts to it. You just need to mix it all together and make sure it's not sticky or wet (if it IS sticky or wet, just add a bit more coconut flour to it).

Step 2: Next thing you do is melt your chocolate in a *bain marie* (a glass bowl on top of a pot of boiling water). I melted 30 grams of 100% dark chocolate but anything above 75% will do the job :-)

Step 3: When the chocolate has melted, dunk your bars in there to coat them.

Step 4: When coated, transfer them to the freezer or fridge (depending on how soon you want them to be ready).

Step 5: BOOM! - DONE! - MUNCH! - WAAAA! = Soft, sharply vanillay, crunchy from the toasted coconut, and m, mm, mmmmmm, tell me you're not in love!

Dark Chocolate & Macadamia Nut Protein Cookies

These protein cookies are vegan. They're also crumbly, soft, rich and with the dark chocolate and macadamia nuts inside them, they're almost sinful! Have a couple alongside a good old cup of coffee and I mmm, experience high-protein cookie heaven :-)

INGREDIENTS

3/4 cup vanilla brown rice protein powder
1 banana
1/2 cup of coconut milk
2 tbsp of unflavored or vanilla pea protein powder
1/4 cup of gluten free oats
4 tbsp of hulled hemp seeds
1 tbsp of coconut oil
20g of 100% dark chocolate (added after blending the above)
2 tbsp of macadamia nuts (added after blending the above)

DIRECTIONS

Blend all the ingredients together except for the chocolate and macadamia nuts which you stir in after blending. Divide the mixture into eight and bake them as cookies on a baking tray at 190 C (374 F) for about 15-20 minutes or until the top has browned and they look ready to munch :-)

MACROS

Per one cookie (out of eight): 120kcals, 10g protein, 7g carbs (2.6g sugars), 6.5g fat (2.8g sat), and 2g fiber!

CHOCOLATE PROTEIN FLAN

INGREDIENTS

1 pint of chocolate milk (I used cartoned chocolate coconut milk but you can sub this with your milk of choice)
1 pack of powdered gelatin (1 pack = 11g)
1/2 cup of chocolate whey protein powder

DIRECTIONS

What you do is heat the milk on the stove until it gets hot-hot but not AAAA-I-JUST-BURNT-MY-%$@&#!-FINGER!-hot, just hot enough to allow you to grab a tablespoon of the stuff and taste it without scalding your mouth. When the milk is ready, pour it in a bowl containing your protein + gelatin and whisk as if your life depended on it. Once you have successfully whisked the whole thing (and no lumps can be found in the milk) pour it into your ramekins, bowls, glasses, and/or mugs and leave them to set overnight. That's it, you're done :-)

MACROS

Per one out of three: 157kcals, 9g protein, 22g carbs (17g sugars), 4g fat (3g sat), and 1g fiber.

A FEW  THANKS

I want to take this opportunity to say thank you to the people who've made proteinpow.com, and subsequently this cookbook, possible. Firstly, I want to thank my husband who's helped me edit this book and fish-out typos from pretty much every page (and many of my blog posts). He's also acted as guinea pig for a lot of my protein experiments, always giving me honest and constructive feedback. I love you crazy amounts, Mr. Sward!!!!

I wish to also thank my dad who opened the gym gates for me and got me hooked on weight-training and nutrition. His advice and jaw-droppingly-amazing cooking skills have always been a source of inspiration and his vision and suggestions for the blog have been invaluable. Thank you for always believing in me and, together with mom, instilling the idea that whatever I set my mind to, I can achieve!

Then, of course, there's Baby - my brother. Thank you for being so supportive, giving me so many new ideas and helpful advice, and following all my posts! Knowing you're reading always makes me smile :-)))))

Lastly (but by no means leastly), I want to thank my friends, dearest Teddy especially, and YOU - the readers and followers of proteinpow. com and facebook.com/proteinpow. You guys have pushed me to constantly experiment, try new foods, and conjure up all sorts of protein magic. I mean it when I say that, without your support and encouragement, none of this would have been possible! So thank you, gracias, ευχαριστώ, tack, merci, спасибо, hvala, danke, takk, obrigada, grazie, dziękuję!